AU?

Understand and Feel Them:

How to Get Rid of Negative Energy

and Create an Amazing Life

By Marta Tuchowska

www.HolisticWellnessProject.com

Disclaimer

A physician has not written the information in this book. This book is for <u>informational and educational purposes</u> only and is not intended as a replacement of any professional medical treatments.

TABLE OF CONTENTS

INTRODUCTION: Feel it! The Concept of Universal Energy and How It Can Change Your Life

Everything in the Universe is connected: people, events, nature, even places. We are all full of energy that we pass along. It doesn't matter if we can or cannot see this energy. It's there. We can feel it. The world and people around us are pulsating with an internal and external energy that we can pick up. We are miniscule drops of water in a vast ocean of universal energy: the universal mind.

It's because of that energy that you feel sad, angry, ecstatic, or motivated. And it's because of that energy that positive or negative things happen in your life.

Have you ever wondered why no matter how hard you try, you cannot achieve your goals? Nothing seems to go right for you? You cannot maintain the relationships you would like?

I know that it can be really frustrating - you try hard, you work hard, you read, you research, and you visualize, yet you cannot find real happiness. You see other people and how they enjoy the gifts of life, yet somehow you feel blocked. Nothing seems to work out for you.

I have been there myself. In fact, 7 years ago I was in a really dark place and no matter how hard I tried, I could not move forward. Now, looking back, I understand that it was a journey and that I had to learn it the hard way. Now, I am grateful for everything that had happened in my life, both good and bad, as it has helped me become who I am today.

Here is one thing to understand. Our own negative energy may be the only thing standing in our way. Our own negative thought processes may be repelling what we want - whether we realize it or not. This is how it works. It's how it always has and always will. No, it's probably not bad luck; it may be as simple as fixing your internal flow of energy. It may be as easy as cleansing your aura and freshening up your thoughts, which will help your aura have a nice, refreshing shower. It all starts in your mind.

You may ask: "Auras- what is she talking about?"

Now, I will ask you to read this book with an open mind. It doesn't matter if you believe in auras or internal energy and it doesn't matter what you want to call it. It doesn't matter if you follow a religion or don't follow anything at all. I respect all the choices you make and I respect your faith. But I am sure that if you are reading this book, you are a seeker. You are a researcher. You have probably noticed that it's all interconnected - your body, mind, and spirit.

My mission is to help you create a healthy body, mind, and spirit. I am a holistic wellness coach. I help people with a myriad of different natural therapies. You see, some people need to take better care of their bodies. They need to focus on a healthy diet and physical activity. Some people already have those healthy habits, but what they need is to work on their mind, motivation, and mindset.

However, sometimes you take care of your body and mind and you wonder, "Is there is anything else I can do?"

I believe that there is. You also need to take care of your spirit, your soul, and your internal energy. Everyone is on a different journey. This is not to say that someone is "more successful" or "more spiritual" because...

Let's throw all that "social proof" stuff away. No judgment, no grades, no numbers. We really need to relax.

Everyone is different, and everyone is trying to find happiness and fulfillment in their own way. Taking care of your body and mind (nutrition, fitness, diets, coaching) is utterly important, but if you want to get better results, you only need to make one decision and get committed to it: work on your soul. Dig deep.

This is not always easy. It can be painful to begin with. Maybe your emotional and spiritual muscles got hurt at some point? The good news is that we can do "physiotherapy and massage for the soul." Yes, for your beautiful soul. By taking care of your internal energy, you will create even more vibrant health, as well as mental and emotional wellbeing. I would like to add that I am not a spiritual guru. I am a seeker, just like you. I am not perfect. I tried to be perfect all my life and the price I had to pay was anxiety and no zest for life. Now I focus on progress rather than perfection. I accepted the fact that life is a journey. The purpose is self-discovery. We need to get committed to creating stronger versions of ourselves.

Taking care of your body, drinking green smoothies, going to the gym, or attending seminars definitely help. I do all of those things. I am not putting down green smoothies or yoga. But sometimes, it's not about spending hours on your yoga mat, and it's not about going on a 10 day green smoothie cleanse or attending a seminar with a motivational guru. I am not saying I don't like them, in fact I love them.

We have all the answers to our problems. It's all about working on our internal energy and first of all realizing what it is and becoming aware of it. In other words, working on your inner energy will help you maximize other healthy lifestyle benefits.

How do I feel? How does it cause me to interact with other people? Why did I say 'yes'? Why did I say 'no'? Why did I feel angry when that person came around? Why did this salesman manage to convince me to buy this stuff? Why did I indulge in alcohol? Why does this person always make me feel uncomfortable?

This is the first step that I recommend. Start asking yourself questions in a gentle, non-judgmental way. Be an observer of your life. Observe and analyze. Then focus on your energy. How did you feel that day? Physically, mentally, and emotionally? Asking yourself questions and being honest with yourself forms one part of self-coaching. Unfortunately, very few people get committed to it.

Our modern, busy agendas do not make it easy, right? I am a modern girl myself. I like to make things easy and uncomplicated. Life is already complicated enough...

In this book, we will go on a journey together. I will show you what you can do to take care of your internal energy. You will learn a lot about yourself. You will be able to make friends with your emotions and your intuition.

Whatever it is that happens to you, you are not alone. You also need to remember that I believe in you. Now you need to believe in yourself.

You have probably heard about the law of attraction. What do you think about it? I myself used to be skeptical about it. However, now I think about it as a 'Law of Internal Energy'. There is also something that I call the 'Law of Action'. It is important that we take action. We cannot just sit down and visualize "stuff". What I also realized is that your personal success depends on the right proportion between the Law of Attraction (or "Law of Internal Energy) and Law of Action. It's not about just taking action to be active and busy. One needs to take meaningful and purposeful action that is in alignment with our real passion and goals, not other peoples' goals.

By the way, what I am saying now are my personal beliefs and opinions that you may or may not agree with. Again, I suggest you read with an open mind. Take what you like and reject things that you don't. I even encourage you to question what you read in this book.

You see, sometimes we may invest too much in the law of attraction and don't take enough action. Usually it results in failure. On the other hand, sometimes we take too much action, but in a 'bad' way. We take action from a point of frustration, doubt, and desperation. Our bodies and minds end up heavily exhausted.

From my experience, the law of attraction works perfectly well if you can create the right proportion between "action" and "attraction". There is no exact rule for that. However, you can analyze your past successes and past failures and ask yourself what you could have done better. Maybe you needed more action? Or maybe you acted too much (and in a bad emotional state)?

First of all, we need to feel good. We need holistic wellness. Trust me, everything else will fall into place.

Let's just quickly discuss the law of attraction. Ok, I can hear the confused voices- why is she talking about it if the book is about auras?

Again, it's all interconnected... Trust me.

Here are the ABC's of what is called the law of attraction.

A. Anything and everything in the universe is made up of energy.
B. Energy trails ideas and thoughts.

C. What you think about, focus on, and put your energy into, you acquire; sometimes in excess.

Your emotions and feelings are energy that works like a magnet. The universal energy matches this by sending equal, echoing energy.

Now, you may already have conquered positive thinking. You may be doing all of the right exercises, using positive affirmations, visualizing the right things, and still not getting what it is that you want. This could be a career goal, a life's dream, or simply looking for love. What the heck is going on here? Well, we have to remember a few things:

1. Our conscious brain is not always in tune with our spiritual mind. The two forms of energy must be in line and in agreement. Sometimes the spiritual mind knows better than our conscious mind.
2. Sometimes our spiritual and conscious mind are on a different time schedule than the universe. It is all about timing.
3. Our own internal energy flow has to be functioning at its best. It has to be free flowing and clean. This is the

one thing we have total control over. This is where the answer to our "problems" usually lies.

We have the ability to cleanse our aura and allow our energy to flow freely throughout our spiritual body. Bad energy needs to be pushed out and blockages must be cleared. Some of those negative things are internal and some are external. Either way, you have the ability to fix it.

A clear aura equals balanced emotions. Have you ever experienced the feeling of connectedness with the here and now? Maybe you did a yoga class or meditated in nature. Maybe you made love to someone you had deep connection with.

Maybe you watched the sunrise on the beach or went to a holistic spa?

In those moments of "here and now," your aura is just the way it should be. You are "here and now." There are no past traumas. There is no worry. No anger.

If only we could always feel that way - we would be in paradise!

No Marta, stop. You're going the wrong way and you are confusing your readers.

You see, Marta, we are in a paradise now. We can train ourselves to always be in the "here and now." We can live a holistic wellness lifestyle.

Ok... This was my inner voice. I needed a positive reminder!

Let's just ask our intellectual minds to analyze this information:

Our system is pumping and vibrating with universal energy. It flows through our chakras and out into our auras. Emotions and ideas change our energy flow and the type of energy that we have, be it positive or negative. When we clear blockages in our internal energy system and cleanse our auras, we will have positive ideas and exude positive energy. Guess what that attracts? You guessed it! Positive things, events, and people. The one thing that we can control is the type of energy we give off. You can have control over your life, relationships, and circumstances! Ok, I know that it may sound a bit hippie dippie at first, but...

The balance of our energy system directly relates to how well we are able to use the law of attraction to our advantage. All we need to do is balance our internal energy. The key to doing this is to learn about auras and chakras, how to clear them, and how to cleanse our energy. This is how we become the captain of our ship instead of the prisoner. I learned this myself and I had no choice but to write this book in order to share with you simple ideas, methods, and tips for doing this.

My life was in shambles. I was 26, a prisoner of dead end jobs, broken relationships, unattained goals, and living in my friend's living room. I would travel or change cities and even countries, thinking that it would solve my problems. I was trying to escape from myself and my thoughts. I wanted to get a second chance. Finally, I quit my job and moved to Italy (I had very little money) thinking I would find my freedom there. But again, I was stuck in a vicious cycle. I knew I wanted something 'different' and I knew I wanted 'balance' but my own mind and emotions were going against me.

There I was, on my 26th birthday, at a trance music festival near Rome. Everyone around me was enjoying the music and the crowd but I just couldn't get into it. I did not want to do drugs or drink alcohol because I knew it would mess me up. I knew that I needed to pull myself together and simply accept the fact that I had made many wrong decisions in my life. I knew I had to re-define my goals and start a journey of authenticity. I felt miserable, sad, disappointed, heart-broken, and also terribly angry with myself. At that time, I had also witnessed some really tragic events in my friend's life (I wanted to help but I couldn't which would make me feel powerless...) and I just realized that everyone was so busy with their own problems and their own agendas. I couldn't blame those around me. I could only blame myself. I also knew

I had to be the one to help myself. No one else could.

I met some really nice people in Italy and they did their best to help me, but it just wasn't the right time or place for me. My negative mind definitely took away so many things I could have enjoyed more.

I am sure you can relate to this. I am sure you know the feeling. You know that you could enjoy life and things around you if it only wasn't for your mind that for some reason chooses to travel to some really dark places.

I always wondered why I had such back luck. Why did I never get to where I wanted to be? Why did it seem like the universe was working against me? The answer was me. It only takes one day to change your life and I hope that this is the day for you! It is *so* possible, achievable, and attainable.

Sometimes you need to ground yourself. You need to be honest with yourself, just like I did on my 26th birthday. On that day, I decided to explore my own failures and learn from them. I decided to leave Italy and spend a couple of months with my family, back in Poland where I am from. It wasn't easy for them, they had to put up with me and my moodiness. However, during that time, I reflected on my mistakes and on my internal energy. I read Marie Diamond's book on Feng Shui and the Law of Attraction. It was actually my little brother who bought this little book for me as a Christmas gift. I finally decided to be the captain of my own ship.

Back in Italy, one of my dear friends gave me her honest feedback which changed my life. She told me that my life was just a wave of unrealistic expectations. I would simply wait for others to do things for me and I would not accept the fact that people had their own agendas. During that time, I decided to design my own life and to have clear goals and objectives.

I would spend lots of time on studying, yoga, and relaxation. I reconnected with some of my old friends. I made enough money to move back to Spain. I decided to take responsibility for my life. From there, things began to change. I began to change, and my internal energy began to change...

Ok, enough about me. Now, it's all about you, not about me.

This book is filled with information to give you a basic understanding of our internal energy system. It breaks down aura color and why it is important to be able to feel auras. But most importantly, I have included tricks and methods to clean your aura that are practical and simple to apply every single day. I always say that practice is much more important than theory. You don't need to be a spiritual guru who can see auras. It's enough if you can just feel them and understand them. You will get an understanding of how to sense, cleanse, and balance your internal energy starting today so that you can start attracting the things that you have always needed and desired. Let's get busy!

Take a few deep breaths, put on some nice relaxing music, burn an incense stick, and let's get started.

CHAPTER 1 What Are Auras and Chakra?

Maybe you are not new to chakras; maybe you have already tried to explore this fascinating topic. If, however, you are a newbie, don't worry. As always, I will make it easy so that you can understand how taking care of your chakras (and understanding them) can take your health and your life to the next level.

Our world is alive with energy, quite literally. Everything in and around us gives off energy of some sort. The atoms in our cells are configured so that each has both negative and positive charges, our own tiny batteries. Our physical bodies are constantly emitting and taking in energy. Every cell has about 1.4 volts of this energy. With 50 trillion cells, the human body is coursing with 700 trillion volts of energy at any given moment. This energy is our life force. It effects our bodily functions, our emotions, and our spirituality. In turn, it is also affected *by* all of these things. Chakras and auras are both ways that we can view, channel, access, and interact with this life energy.

The power plants, or hubs, for our life energy are our chakras. Chakra means *spinning wheel* in Sanskrit. These spinning wheels of light and energy are usually characterized as a row of colored circles that run from the head to the genitals. Chakras, in reality, are actually spinning vortexes of color and light that radiate from the center of the body, through both the front and the back.

There are seven main chakras. Each channels the flow of energy through our beings. Chakras are the regulators and gate keepers of our life force. The level at which our chakras are functioning is a reflection of how we choose to handle circumstances in life. Our thoughts, feelings, and how we generally view the world around us determine how open or closed our chakras are.

Chakras are an extension of our awareness. They have more mass than auras, but less than the body. Even though they are part of our consciousness, chakras play a part in the physical processes of the body. Every chakra is linked with an endocrine gland. Each is also connected to a plexus, which is a network of nerves.

Therefore, since every chakra covers a different area of the body, some physical ailments can be directly related to a chakra that is out of balance. This is why it's so important to master the art of relaxation, meditation, and mindfulness. Ever since I decided to take more breaks from work and even do "technology detoxes" from time to time, my productivity, focus, and overall happiness have skyrocketed.

Think about it...

Every chakra vortex is made up of smaller vortexes. Each small vortex has a different rate of vibration and a different hue. They all combine together to make a certain tone and color when they are balanced. Each mini-chakra represents one of the many aspects of that chakra. If one thing is missing in your life, it can throw off the balance of the entire chakra. Not only does each chakra need to remain balanced, all of them must be in synch for the body, mind, and spirit to function optimally.

Crown — Sahasrara
Third Eye — Ajna
Throath — Vishuddha
Heart — Anahata
Solar Plexus — Manipura
Sacrum — Svadhisthana
Root — Muladhara

<u>Seven Chakras</u>:

1. Root/Red: This chakra is responsible for feelings of security and survival (finances, food, and shelter). It is located at the bottom of the spine, near the tailbone. It regulates the testes and the ovaries.

2. Sacral/Orange: This chakra is responsible for pleasure, sexuality, and happiness. It is located right below the belly button. It regulates the pancreas.

3. Solar Plexus/Yellow: This chakra is responsible for self-confidence, self-empowerment, and self-respect. It is located in the upper abdomen. It regulates the adrenals.

4. Heart/Green: This chakra is responsible for love, joy, validation, and peace. It is located in the center of the chest. It regulates the thymus.

5. Throat/ Blue: This chakra is responsible for the ability to communicate and express thoughts and feelings. It is located in the throat. It regulates the thyroid.

6. Third Eye/Indigo: This chakra is responsible for clairvoyance, decision making, and imagination. It is located right in the center of the forehead. It regulates the pituitary gland.

7. Crown/Violet: This chakra is located on top of the head. It is responsible for spirituality and beauty.

Chakras can be fine-tuned through many different avenues. Just like a car, we need to do some maintenance work for chakras from time to time. It is important to keep the chakras open and functioning at the highest level possible in order to achieve mental clarity and spirituality to the fullest, and to promote excellent health and emotional wellness. This can be done through meditation, crystal balancing, music, EFT, yoga, color and aromatherapy, Reiki, breathing techniques, guided visualizations, affirmation, and quite a few more. One of the most fun and interesting parts of learning about chakras is finding the techniques that you like the most and which works best for your body. When I first took interest in chakras, I went overboard. I became too obsessed. I worried myself so much thinking whether or not what I eat, do, or think about will make my chakras over-active or under-active. It was so bad that I was actually causing them, and myself, more harm than good. This is why I advise you not to go overboard. You don't have to apply all these techniques at once. Sometimes it's much better to focus just on one thing, master it and make it your habit.

It's just like with physical workouts. Some people get too focused on getting more information that they never have chance to apply it. In this day and age, there is what I call "information overload". I think that too much information can make us anxious. Sometimes, you may be better off if you just focus on one diet, or one workout (but do it every day), or one business model.

The same applies to your beautiful chakras. You may just pick up one thing, one tiny thing, and go from there. Then, of course, you can gradually explore new ways of balancing your auras and chakras and practice them more. Always remember to stick to what you enjoy doing and what works for you. I personally love writing and creating. Writing helps me get focused, and I also feel fulfilled as I hope that my books can help or inspire someone. Whatever it is that you love doing - it doesn't matter if you do it professionally or as a hobby, try to do it more. You see, any type of creative activity helps us feel more balanced.

Now that you have an understanding of what a chakra is, it will be easier for you to grasp the concept of what an aura is and how they interrelate. The chakras are essentially energy gates of the aura. They keep our auras luminous and vivid, and when they are in balance, they will keep us healthy and happy. Chakras are a powerful tool to attain true holistic wellness, and I hope that you investigate them further.

How chakras radiate energy into the aura:

Our life-force energy is taken into the chakra via its inward bound vortex, where it is then transported into the main orb of the chakra. This central area is what we tend to define as the chakra. From there, it is transported through the meridians and the central channel (the current that passes the energy through each of the chakras vertically). As life-energy flows through the body, it is picked up by each person's DNA and passed along to the nervous and endocrine systems. At the same time, our DNA is emitting the energy all around the outside of the body, creating the aura.

Auras:

'Aura' sounds like a mystical, supernatural, hocus pocus bunch of non-sense to some. In all actuality, the aura is very real. It is simply the natural energy of your body, put out by the chakras, radiating around you. Auras are our own personal energy field. The world and people around us are affected by the energy of the aura. If you pay close attention, you can feel the energy of another person when they are close to you, or in your personal space (aura). Some people make you feel nice. Some people make you feel angry. Some people make you feel energized and some can make you feel tired or you even feel like running away from them. Why? It's because of their auras.

Auras can actually be seen as an 'egg' of color glowing around the human body. The color of one's aura is determined by the strongest chakras, although the color is a mixture of all your chakra light energy. Everyone's aura can be seen as any one of the colors in the rainbow. They appear as different hues and shades, each one having a different meaning regarding emotion, spirituality, and health. The colors will be covered in greater detail in the following chapter.

Auras are comprised of an equal amount of layers, regardless of color. Layers differ in deepness and transparency. Most often, seven layers are seen, although it is possible for certain people to decipher nine. There is a possibility that more layers exist, but have not currently been defined.

Each chakra corresponds to a layer of the aura and are listed from 1-7, from close to the body and moving outward. Oddly enough (no pun intended), layers 1,3,5, and 7 have a tendency to be more well configured, while 2,4, and 6 are more iridescent, fluctuating, and fluid. The higher the number, the higher the vibration is. This causes a current of energy that moves vertically, pulsing up and out to the perimeter of the aura. The healthier the individual and the more open the chakras, the further the aura can extend off of the body.

1. **Etheric:**

   Ether is the space that is between energy and matter, from the planets to the stars, and even the space between atoms. This layer ranges from a ¼ inch to 2 inches away from the edge of our physical body. The etheric layer is the medium to which our own skin is affixed. It is made up of little, delicate threads of energy that are interwoven around the body. It is almost a copy of your skin, yet it is made of energy. Flickers of energy travel through this matrix, sparkling as they flow. Many well-practiced aura viewers can see this web of energy. Beginners may only view a muted, blurry, transparent vapor, kind of like you see coming off of the ground on an extremely hot day. Many people have seen it, even if they have never tried to view an aura. It can be seen as anything from grey or blue fog to a novice, to sparks of blue or grey light by the well-trained eye. Active people tend to have more of a grey color, while those who are more inactive have more of a blue coloring.

   The Etheric Layer is interconnected with the Root Chakra and what we experience through our five senses. This means that both physical pain and pleasure have an effect on the Etheric Body. What we eat and the way that we exercise (or lack of exercise) has an influence on it as well. The way that we feel (or vibe) other's energy also takes place in the Etheric Body. The energy here throbs at a rate near 20 cycles every 60 seconds.

2. Emotional:

Aptly named, this layer deals with our feelings and emotions. The Emotional Layer reaches out 1-3 inches from the physical body. It is a fluid layer that permeates all of the other layers. The unformulated flames of color do not resemble the shape of our physical body. The colors of the Emotional Body fluctuate in response to the emotion being felt at the time. The colors range from vivid, thanks to positive emotion, to muddy, in response to negative emotion. It is possible to see every color in this layer, and it is usually the first layer of color that someone learns to see.

Intertwined with the Sacral Chakra, the Emotional Body is connected to how we perceive ourselves, and how those perceptions make us feel. In order to keep this layer thriving, it is important to vent and feel those emotions, regardless of what they are. Do not hold them in or ignore them. You need to have this 'emotional peeling' or 'emotional shower'. You see, emotional dirt can finally manifest itself in physical diseases and imbalances.

3. Mental:

Like the Etheric Layer, this layer is more defined and configured. It is found 3-8 inches away from the physical body. The Mental Body is usually seen as yellow or gold in color, and is brightest between the head and the shoulders. The radiance of the light in this layer is brightest while concentrating and focusing on a mental task. Sometimes sparks and splotches of colors are seen when one creates repetitive thought patterns. These color differences are dictated by how a person is connected emotionally to their thought processes.

Our Mental Layer interacts with the Solar Plexus Chakra. It is interrelated with both left and right brain capabilities. The equal use of both sides of the brain, logical and imaginative, will keep the Mental Body in good health. Daydreaming, lucid dreaming, the active use of the imagination, active learning, and the quest for knowledge are all things that we can do to achieve this well-being. The Mental Layer is susceptible to serious destruction if one stays in a state of negativity or cynical thinking for too long.

4. **Astral:**

This vaporous layer is full of color, reaching out 1-1 ½ feet outside of the body. The Astral Layer is where we create astral cords that connect us to others, whether they are positive or negative, current or previous connections. The Astral Body is the area of the aura where we pick up on the vibes (vibrations) of others. It is usually bathed in a pinkish color due to the formation of romantic or platonic relationships that are created. Many chakras can be seen in the Astral Layer, but usually have a pink hue.

The Astral Layer is a long-term collection of how we feel about ourselves, on both an emotional and intellectual level. It is the connection linking experiences. The Astral Body rules visualization, dreaming, and hallucinating. You are mentally aware of this part of yourself, but at the same time, you can still come into contact with other levels of reality. The Astral Body allows us to project and be in two places at the same time.

The Astral Layer is connected to the Heart Chakra. This connection links us to relations with others, and how these associations have an influence on our emotions. The way to keep this layer functioning at its best is by keeping healthy, encouraging, constructive relationships with people and the world around us.

5. **Etheric Template:**

This layer is located around 1 ½-2 feet outside of the body. The Etheric Template is actually a structured blueprint or master plan of everything that is alive on the physical level. It is a negative of the Etheric Layer, a dark blue background with thin, light energy streaks. When something is wrong with the Etheric Layer, you can go into your Etheric Template to find out how to rebalance.

This template is connected to the Throat Chakra, the place where noise is turned into matter. The Etheric Template is where divine will and the power of manifesting your will into existence are formed. Devine will is established by our inner, higher self and is the greatest longing for a direction in our existence that will serve a greater good. By aligning our free and divine wills, we can have a healthy, vivid Etheric Template

Layer. When these two wills are not lined up, this layer will still have energy lines, but they will not be as plentiful nor as bright. This will cause you to feel as if you are wandering in life without purpose. By using the power of manifestation in relation to your divine and free will, you can rebalance this layer by changing your reality and existence.

6. **Celestial:**

While the Etheric Layer is more of a physical form of the higher self, the Celestial Layer is the emotional form of the higher self. It is located about 2-2 ¾ feet outside of the body. The colors in the Celestial Body are iridescent and pastel, almost like a bubble or an abalone shell. In this layer, we have a connection to a higher power and generate unconditional love that attaches us to other physical beings. It generates energy, much like a star or the sun, radiating outward.

The Celestial Body is associated with the Third Eye Chakra. It reflects our connections, on a spiritual level, with the universe. We can keep this layer healthy by practicing meditation, present moment awareness, and by pondering religion, spirituality, or the philosophies of reality and existence. The Celestial Layer is where we view the divine and spiritual nature within ourselves and in those around us. It also connected to each individual's awareness of the divine, and how sensitive and open we are to the spiritual realm.

7. **Ketheric Template:**

Extending 2 ½-3 feet away from the body, this layer is where we become aware of the fact that we are one with our higher power and the universe. Its outer edge is the toughest, most durable layer. The Ketheric Layer is oval in shape, like an egg. Comprised of thin, pulsating golden threads, it also supplies the energy that runs through the spine, powering the entire body. The higher self fills the Ketheric Body, and this can be seen by way of a gold glow. It is the intellectual layer of the spiritual realm. Here in the Ketheric Layer we are joined with the universal mind and are able to comprehend it, as well as being able to understand past lives.

The Ketheric Body is intertwined with the Crown Chakra, and connects us to the universal mind. We can keep this layer healthy by understanding, and having insights regarding our place in the universal mind and our connection to the divine. This is achieved by having contact with a higher power and having spiritual experiences. We can strengthen the Ketheric Body by constantly seeking out divine wisdom, knowledge, and ideas.

The above descriptions of the Auric Layers included ways to keep them individually strong and healthy. There are also other ways to keep up with your auric health.

- Just like your physical body, your auric bodies need a checkup. It is wise to have a complete aura reading by a professional. You will learn if, and where, you have gaps, rips, or warped areas in your aura. All of these problems could be potential signs of health issues. Misshapen areas in certain parts of the aura can point to where an ailment or physical damage may be hiding. To illustrate, a rip in the aura near the shoulder might signal joint problems. A depression near the kidneys could be signaling tumors or disease. Warped spots in the aura can be present due to emotional issues as well. A deformity near the ribcage might be a red flag signaling pain, distrust, or sadness due to current situations or caused by traumatic past experiences.

Once your aura has been read, there are many avenues to take in order to fix your energy flow. The first step toward auric health is to have it read. There is nothing to be scared about. It's fun.

- Energy from others is taken into our aura. This can be good, if the other person has positive energy. Negative energies are what we need to be wary of, as they can have a very detrimental effect on our aura. We have quick, auric run-ins with people all the time, but by being around someone all the time, or by being in close proximity with a lot of people, negative energies are more easily absorbed. Sometimes, you may absorb someone's negative energy even if you interact with them online, or haven't directly interacted with them at all. Yes, I know it sounds scary, but I am sure it has happened to you at least once. Somebody may be sending you negative thoughts and energy, consciously or not. If you think that your aura has been disturbed and has ingested negative energy, there is hope! There are purifying rituals that can rid your aura of negativity. Here are two examples of great visualization rituals that will cleanse your aura. The following rituals will also help you feel more relaxed, centered, and focused. You can thank me later.

1. **Shower:**
   - Close your eyes. Visualize a shower: any kind, shape, size, even a waterfall. Decide on a shower that will allow you to feel comfortable and clean. Use your imagination and sense to experience everything: the smells, the texture under your feet, and the sound of the water.

   - Step under the water and feel the water rush over your skin. Take in everything: the temperature, the smell of the water, the rush of the cleansing water over your skin. Feel the negative energy rinsing right off of your skin as the water runs down you.

   - Stay in your shower until all of the negativity has washed away. Watch as the water goes down the drain or rushes away the in pool under the waterfall. The negative energy is going with it. Remain there until you are relaxed and clean.

2. **Bubble:**

- Go to a quiet, relaxing, comfortable spot. While lying down, slowly count to twenty with your eyes closed. Imagine, in your mind's eye, a large pink bubble quite a few feet above you.
- Slowly, use all of your energy and imagination to visualize transporting all of the negative energy that is congesting your aura up and away from you into the bubble.
- Do this as long as it takes to feel released from the negativity. Once you feel the "all clear," allow the bubble, full of the negative energy, higher and higher up into the air until you see it disappear. Now that it is gone, you are free of that negativity.

- Negative human energy is not the only kind of negative energy that can mess up your aura. The negative energy in any given location can be absorbed into the aura. Auras are prone to taking on negativity from environments like: jails, graveyards, haunted locations, various types of medical facilities, locations of frequent drug use, and many more. Try to keep your time at these kinds of places short and infrequent. Use cleansing rituals after you leave. You can keep absorption to a minimum by waving your arms around, dissipating and pushing the negative energy churning around you away. Sage (the white variety) can also be used to strengthen and stimulate your own aura's positive energy. Black tourmaline is also an easy way to fend off negative energy. Some people carry it in their pocket, but a fun way to keep it with you is to have a piece of jewelry that contains it.

- Knowing that the physical body is related to the auric bodies, keeping the physical health in shape will also keep our aura vivid and brilliant. Just as the circulation of the physical body is detrimental to health, so is the circulation of energy important to auric health. Eating well can help certain chakras to open up. The Heart Chakra responds to dark leafy greens. Healthy grains like quinoa will help to ground the Root Chakra. The Third Eye and Crown Chakras respond well to the antioxidant properties found is dark berries and dark grapes. Not only can we eat our way to physical health, we can eat our way to auric health!

- One more thing you can do to keep your aura functioning at its best is to spend time in nature. Nature is full of positive energy. Spending time outdoors will help to relax the body and mind and rejuvenate the spirit. Amp up your aura and allow nature to cleanse and heal it. Even something as simple as taking a barefoot walking in the grass or dirt is very cleansing and will ground you. Relax in the sea, let the waves crash into you. Float down a river or wade in a stream. These natural water sources have a very cleansing quality. Nature will allow you to feel free, and give you a more positive perspective, which will in turn brighten and strengthen your aura.

"Just living is not enough... one must have sunshine, freedom, and a little flower."- Hans Christian Andersen

www.holisticwellnessproject.com

Nature is the best healer, the best spa. And the good news is that it's free.

Leave your office, switch off your mobile device and tablet. Be in nature. Just be. You will feel so much better and as a result, you will work better. Human beings were not made to spend long days and nights in front of PC screens...

Even if you are a city person, you can still spend 1 day a week in nature, right? Or even 1-2 days a month? You need to recharge your batteries. Slow down. Everyone around you will appreciate it. Why? Because they will love your new energy!

CHAPTER 2 Embrace the Power of Colors

The aura cannot be pretended. It cannot be influenced by your own personal stereotypes, the stereotypes of others, your routines and habitual nature, artificial behavior, or fake mannerisms. The aura is a mirror image of *the genuine spirit* and personality of any given person. It shows *our true nature.*

Many people put in a considerable amount of work to get back to their true self. They put aside all of the fake, shallow, unnatural habits and stereotypes that are picked up both subconsciously and consciously during their lives. They strive for awareness, consciousness, and wakefulness. Their true self is almost always apparent. Many other people are so absorbed in putting on appearances, so engrossed in the habits and mannerisms that they have taken on, that is difficult to see their true nature by observing them and being around them. In some cases, it is just not possible to gauge their real personality. The only way to do so is to read their aura, because artificial character is not reflected in the aura.

Thanks to technology and science, there are ways to actually see the aura without much effort. Not everyone has access to this technology, or the people who use it. This book focuses on seeing (and feeling) on the aura yourself, or by someone who does not have this technology, which is why the focus will be on seeing the aura with the eye. Auras do surround the entirety of the body, but are usually easiest to see around the head and shoulder area. We will discuss the colors and their meanings based on this area of the body.

Before we investigate the actual meanings behind certain colors, here are some added tips when reading auric color:

1. Most auras have 1-2 principal colors. They are known as "auric pairs" and will sometimes be the person's favorite color.
2. The more vivid the aura, the more aware and spiritual the person most likely is. The more evenly that the energy is spread out in the aura more likely it is that the person is in good health.
3. The aura is not only comprised of dominant colors. They also contain changing flickers, sparks, or flame-like flashes that come and go. These are usually contemplations, feelings, ideas, and wants. The color of these flashes usually falls under one of the definitions

below, usually as a thought of the feeling denoted by the color.

Red: An aura that is principally red usually signals a person who is very concerned with material possessions and physical appearance. Flashes of red usually indicate thoughts that are material items or something physical about the body.

Pink (a combination of purple and red): An aura that is pink is a combination of purple (highest frequency) and red (lowest frequency). Pink auras signal a person who has a balance of materialism and spirituality. A few people may be seen with a halo that is yellow and a huge exuding pink aura. This is a very rare dominant aura color and is usually only seen as a thought, temporarily.

Orange: An aura that has orange as its dominant color. Orange is inspirational and fascinating. People with orange auras are inspirational and authoritative. They usually have the power to control people. When orange is a dominant color, usually a gold halo can be seen, denoting a powerful spiritual instructor.

An orange flicker usually represents a thought that the person is having in regard to commanding others.

Yellow: Someone with a yellow aura is joyful, charitable, and free. A yellow halo will only be seen on a person who is a spiritual instructor, as it signals extraordinary spiritual growth. The thickness of the halo will be one inch or less. The yellow halo is an auric pair with the violet brow chakra. Those who are working toward a high level of spirituality focus attention on this chakra because they are concentrating on divine thoughts and ideas. Yellow flickers of thought signal ideas and feelings of jubilation and serenity.

Green: People who have green auras are usually healers by nature. The more dominant and clear the green aura, the more practiced or efficient the healer. Green auras usually have a "green thumb" as well and are great at gardening. Being near a green aura will bring you tranquility and peace. When you see green flashes, this signals that the person is in a position of restoration and relaxation.

Turquoise: Auras of this color indicate that the person is a great at multitasking, they're high-energy, and have great organizational skills. They like to think about many things at the same time and have great influence over others. People with turquoise auras make great supervisors in the workplace because they go over their objectives and visions, motivating their subordinates instead of just demanding compliance. Turquoise flashes and flames indicate a thought or idea related to organization or persuading others.

Blue: People who have dominant blue auras are tranquil, well-adjusted, and sensible. They are survivalists and can go run off to live in a cave or bunker. They would be happy to live off of the land. Blue flickers usually indicate thoughts about survival and the relaxation of the nervous system. A bright, vivid blue supersedes any auric color. It is usually seen when someone is telepathically accepting or conveying communication.

Purple: Purple is never a dominant aura color, they're only seen as flickers of thoughts. They represent exceptionally divine thoughts.

Darker, Smokey Colors

Brown: Worrisome, disturbing, selfish, greedy, materialistic thoughts that oppose divinity and spirituality.

Grey: Morbid, discouraging, and depressing thoughts. May show unclear motives or the existence of a dark side.

Mustard-like: Signals discomfort, hardship, rage, or resentment.

White: The color white signifies problems in the aura. White color is like a racket, compared to the melodious pitch that an aura should have. White indicates discord in the person. Before a person passes away, the aura turns white. That is why, historically, death is characterized by white, instead of black.

The understanding of auric colors will help you to understand more about your true-self, and the true nature of others. In dealing with ourselves, it helps us to see areas of improvement and where we really are on our path to enlightenment. It can be the first step in figuring out what your strong points really are and the potential to use them to the best of your ability. Not only that, but you may see an indicator for illness, or negative energy that you could have picked up from someone else, or that you have inside of yourself. When dealing with others, our understanding of auric colors can help us to enlighten others about their true nature and possible physical and emotional health concerns. It also allows us to see past fake personalities in order to determine the kinds of people we want to allow into our lives.

CHAPTER 3 Can You Read Auras?

Being able to see an aura is a very practical, insightful tool. It will help you to learn more about yourself and those around you. For most people, it takes a bit of training and practice to learn how to see an aura. There are many different approaches and tips that will allow you to train your eyes and your consciousness to make it possible. Another approach is to feel them and understand them. Once you have started analyzing your behavior and emotions (as well as other people's), it will become natural for you.

Auras can be difficult to see at first, but once you realize that you can do it and it clicks, you will be able to repeat the process. Naturally, it is easy for kids to see auras. Babies can see them as well because they have clear, balanced chakras.

There are many ways to learn how to see auras. If you are not a "natural," do not worry, with practice you can learn how to train your eyes to see them. The techniques I have listed will aid you in figuring out how. They will also help you practice and hone your skills. Some of the methods are for use on people and others for objects. Try them all and see what works for you. For some, it may take more work, but it is possible for everyone to learn how to see auras. These are the exercises that I learned from one of my massage therapy teachers. She knew everything about auras; in fact she would always know how her students felt. She could actually see auras naturally - this is a gift she was blessed with ever since she could remember.

1. Other People/White Background
   - Put your subject in front of a white background with nothing on it. Make sure that there are no shadows. Using a colored background will make it harder.
   - Pick a spot on the person to focus on. It will allow your peripheral vision to take over. You will be concentrating on one spot, and this will allow the rest of your vision to relax. Indian culture suggests that you focus on the third eye, right between the eyebrows.

- Stare at this spot for a minute or longer, without losing focus. This will take practice. Every time you find your gaze moving, refocus.
- After a minute, become aware of your peripheral vision. You must do this without taking your concentration off of your focal point. This too will take practice, and if you lose your focal point, refocus and start over. When you do this, you should notice that the border between the body and the background has a glowing color to it. It should be a color different than the rest of the backdrop.

The longer that you focus your vision, the brighter it should become. By focusing on one spot, you are increasing your visual sensitivity to the aura. You can also allow your eyes to go out of focus, if you know how. This will allow you to pick up on other visual cues you may not have noticed.

Extra tips: Once you achieve seeing the color, have your subject shift their body from side to side. You should see their aura moving as well. Do not work on focusing for too long. Only engage in the practice for a couple of minutes at a time. Let your eyes rest in between moments of focus. If you are not seeing the aura clearly, try playing your subject's favorite music. This may invigorate their aura, allowing it to be seen more clearly.

2. Yourself/White Background/Hand:

- Use a white wall or a sheet of white paper.
- Make sure that the lighting is natural: the sun or a candle. Do not do this at night. Practice in a room that is shaded from direct sunlight. If it is too bright, it will not work properly.
- Hold up a hand against the white background and let your eyes relax. Focus on the tips of the fingers or allow your eyes to go out of focus (this works best for me). Slowly but surely, you will see a clear or blue-ish glow start to form around your hand. Keep your gaze steady, and refocus or relax again as necessary. Eventually the brightness will turn into a color.
- Decide exactly what colors you are seeing.

Extra tips: Sometimes you will see an "after image" or a negative looking effect. Do not base your auric color on this. You will be able to tell if it is a negative image if you look away from your subject matter and wherever you look you will see the same image inversely. Just like when you stare at a bright light for a long period of time and see it no matter where you look for a minute or so afterward. Also, do not worry if you start to see the color and it disappears quickly. Blinking of the eyes and loss of focus is common.

Afterwards, it is helpful and fun to take a white piece of paper and draw an outline of your body. Using colored pencils, pastels, whatever you like, to sketch out the colors you see. You can keep them on hand for your own personal reference, or just to show others.

Do not get discouraged if you do not see anything right away. You have to relax, practice, and train your eyes. Try these exercises when you are calm and in a place free of distraction. Make sure that you do this in an environment where you are completely undistracted. If sunlight is not working for you, use a dark room only illuminated with candlelight.

3. Yourself/Mirror
   - Have large mirror about four feet in front of you. Try to make sure that the background behind

you is white. You should see to it that there are as few shadows as possible. The lighting should be constant and soft.

- Follow the same instructions as above when you used your hand.

Do this for 10 15 minutes every day. This will help you to train your eyes to see auras.

Extra tips: Once you are able to see your inner-aura, the blueish white glow, you can try your hand at seeing color. As in the previous exercise, place yourself in front of the mirror. Focus on seeing that same inner aura again, but now, try to concentrate on the border of that glow. With practice, the glow will grow wider. You should eventually be able to see color start to border the edge, and it may be hazy, or dim at first. This is how you will be able to see the color of the middle aura. It will take time, but step by step and with practice, you should become more comfortable with it.

From here, you can move on to seeing the shape of the aura. You will need all the materials in the exercises above, but this time a full length mirror would be more helpful. Find the border, your white glow, and relax your vision to see the other colors. Start with your head, and when you lose focus, simply bring it back. It is a practice of refocusing your attention.

As you get more skilled, you can train your eyes to see the aura in front of the body, not only around it. Once you are focused, follow the aura from one side of the body to another. Across the top of the head is a good place to try. Move from one shoulder, over the head, to the other shoulder. After you master that, try looking at the front of yourself, even down your torso, groin, and legs.

4. Yourself/Fingers
   - Place your hands together and press the tips of your index fingers together. Pull them apart just a bit. Concentrate your gaze in between them. You are trying to focus on waves of energy passing between them, kind of like heat waves on a warm asphalt parking lot. Relax your vision every so often and let them go out of focus intermittently.

   - Another option using your digits is to stretch one of your arms out directly in front of you. Curl your hand into a fist, thumb facing up. Move the thumb

to eye-level. Now, concentrate you gaze o1
Hold your focus without blinking for as lo1
possible. If performed correctly, you shoulc ⌐ ɑᴜɪe
to make out wisps of energy, right there at the tip.

5. Trees

- Trees are large and produce an aura that can be huge, strong, and clearly visible. Try to do this around dawn or in the evening. Pick a tree that is tall, broad, and stands alone. Stand approximately 20 feet away from it. Focus on the tree's outline. It should be a hazy, green/grey color. You will see this outline between the sky and the tree most often faintly at first, then once you have caught a glimpse of it, let your eyes go out of focus a bit or squint slightly. Practice for as long as you need to. You can try other trees as well.

6. Plants

- Find a plant that is still. Potted plants work well for this exercise. Find a spot to focus your attention on, either near the top or the base. Allow your eyes to relax and go out of focus. This can also be accomplished by focusing slightly beyond the plant.

Slowly, the white aura of the plant should begin to appear. You may not see the same colors that you would when reading a person's aura, but it is still a useful practice. It will help to train your eyes to see other auras.

Practicing Tips and Tricks

1. Practice your sensing skills. Be aware of how you feel around others. What "vibe" are they giving you? Are they leeching from your energy or adding to it? While paying attention to their energy, focus on your breathing. Note what your physical senses are telling you, and how they are making your mind and body feel. Practice picturing the color this person makes you feel. You may not always be correct, but it is a great way to start sensing aura. Visualization and sensation go hand in hand.

2. Practice using your peripheral vision. This is an ability that most people have, but because we do not always use it in everyday life, it must be strengthened. It is also an area of sight that has not incurred as much damage as the rest of the eye. You can practice for a minute or so at a time by focusing your sight on one spot. It will

heighten your sensitivity, and you will notice a big difference in your focus in the far corners of your vision.

3. Practice with colors. Find a white solid background, like a wall, and make sure the lighting is mellow, with no direct glare. Wrap a book in a bright primary colored paper and stand it up on a table, facing you, white wall in the background. Place yourself a few feet away. Take a few cleansing breaths with your eyes closed, open them looking directly at your subject. Practice on focusing on the border of it, even a little bit past it. You should start to see a thin, glowing border. Keep your focus and you should notice it turning a greenish-yellow. This can be done with many objects and colors. It will help you train your eyes to see color that our everyday vision does not always pick up. When you lose focus during a practice such as this, do not worry, you are not doing it wrong. Stay relaxed and focused. The more you do it, the better your eyes will be at balancing themselves this way.

4. Quick fixes: honing your aura reading skills can be done all the time. There are little things that you can do anywhere. Gauge the aura of a customer or co-worker. Focus on them and you may notice a difference in it as

they become angry, frustrated, comfortable, or pleased. When at the beach, look at the border of the water on the horizon. The crest of a crashing wave is also electrifying.

Nature holds many aura-fying sights which, if we remain still and focused, can blow our minds. A simple man-made key can be a wonder. Hold it in your hand for fifteen minutes. Seal your energy into it. Put it down, and visualize your energy in the key. You should actually be able to see your emotion fixed onto it.

Pay attention to how people walk, talk, and express themselves. After a while, you will even be able to feel and sense person's aura from e-mails or text messages they send you. After devoting some time to working with your internal energy, you will also develop more empathy towards other people. This in turn can help you in both your personal and professional life.

You will no longer complain about managers, bosses, clients, or significant others and their choices. You see, you were one of their choices as well. Thanks to energy work, you will take more responsibility for your actions and your thoughts.

Remember

Do not lose faith if you are not picking it up right away. As we move through life, some people become desensitized to the process. We have to strengthen and train that ability. With any training comes practice, of course! You can develop the skill to see auras, just do not give up. 15 to 20 minutes of practice goes a long way. Try to practice every day. The ability to sense energy takes time. As you take little steps, you will gain more confidence in your abilities. Confidence plays a huge part in the ability to see auras, just like in case of everything else you wish to master. You need to act from the point of confidence, not from the point of doubt or frustration.

Again, please keep in mind that you can also focus on feeling auras and understanding them. Try to sympathize with yourself and others. Understand where you are coming from and where those around you are coming from. Think what their story may be and how it affects their behavior. Don't judge. Observe and accept. It will open the gate to more happiness and spiritual abundance.

CHAPTER 4 Balancing Auras for Physical and Emotional Health

Teaching people how to achieve *holistic balance* is just my favorite thing to do!

Before I move forward, I would like to give you my definition of balance. Yours may be different. After all, we are all different. It's not about being right or wrong, we are all right. It's about sticking to things and beliefs that work for us and help us during our journey of self-discovery. Again, take what you like and reject the rest.

There are many definitions of balance. However, I believe that real balance does not really exist. To me, balance is not about relaxing all day long. Too much relaxation can do more harm than good. Think about it - what if you just get too lazy? Some people may think that balance is achieved by sticking to 50/50 rule: spend a certain amount of hours working and a certain amount of hours relaxing.

This is something I may agree with, but every day is different. Sometimes, we need to follow the flow and listen to our inner voice. For example, sometimes in order to stay balanced we need to increase our working hours, and sometimes we need to relax more. There is no fixed rule for that. Your energy changes every day, and so does your aura - this is why!

Here is my definition of balance, and it works fantastically for me. It's basically about continuously working on your body, mind, and soul so that you can make progress in all areas of your life - not just one. I sometimes see people focusing too much on finances (which I can understand, I have also been "guilty" of it, I am not judging or anything, I am just saying) and they neglect health and family. Or some people focus too much on their social life (going out, drinking) and then they wonder why they can't attract wealth or are not healthy enough.

Balance is about realizing where you need to focus on more NOW. It may change next week or next month. It's not that you always need to put the exact same amount of energy to all areas of life.

This is why it is just as important for us to keep up our energy body (or spiritual wellness) as it is for us to keep up our physical body, yet many people neglect it. Our life energy not only affects our physical and mental health (and vice-versa), it also brings things into our life, and possibly repels others. Keeping our auras bright and healthy allows us to stay in great emotional and physical shape as well. Holistic wellness can also be thought of as holistic balance. Sadly, especially in this day and age, our life-energy body can become neglected. Now that you are aware of this, you have the power to fix it easily.

The balancing and cleansing process will not only help you to feel energized, think clearly, have control over your emotions, it will help you to deflect negative energy and pass positive energy to others. Not only is it possible to pick up negative energies from others, we can also produce it in ourselves. Negative thoughts about ourselves and past experiences create bad energy. The wrong diet, lack of exercise, or use of drugs and alcohol can also taint the aura with negative energy. This causes an imbalance or blockage in the flow of our life energy. Besides, people oftentimes use alcohol, drugs, tobacco, or even food to try to feel better and forget about their problems. Unfortunately it creates the vicious circle pattern. The best way to "stop the madness" and break the vicious cycle is to at least try to feel good from the inside and embrace holistic wellness.

We know what happens when our energy is blocked or unbalanced. The aura will suffer as well as our physical being. You can become sick, feel lethargic, nervous, disheartened, or emotionally and mentally unstable. It is possible to balance and clear our flow of energy and achieve wellness by cleansing the aura.

There are many different methods of aura cleansing available. Most are not super complicated, in fact most are super practical and easy to use! Many of them are also beneficial to your physical health, so why not try them? Did you know that even drinking 12 glasses of spring or purified water a day will help to purify the aura? I find that using all of these methods in combination works quite well. You will enjoy engaging in these aura cleansing techniques and finding out which ones work best for you.

1. Bathe in sea salt. Yes, something as simple as taking a bath in dissolved sea salt is very cleansing for your aura.

We have to wash our spiritual body just like we was our physical body.

This type of bath takes away negative energy while strengthening the aura. Sea salt builds a type of barrier that protects against negative energy. Sea salt is very grounding and will pull out undesirable spiritual energy from the skin. Water is purifying by nature and will cleanse our positive energy. After a sea salt bath, you will be left with a protected and cleansed aura.

Different people conduct this bathing ritual in various ways. The most important things to include are a previously bathed body, sea salt, and an undisturbed period of time. 15 to 30 minutes is recommended. Your favorite essential oils can be added, you can burn incense, play calming music, or a guided meditation.

- Fill your bathtub with warm water and dissolve a cup or two of sea salt into it. I relax my entire body, a section at a time, bottom to top.
- Next, I visualize all of my stress, worry, self-doubt, and negative feelings brought on by others being sucked out of my body through the skin.

- Try to make sure all of your body is submerged at one point or another.
- When you are done, get out of the bath knowing you are clean and free of any negativity.
- If using essential oils, add a few drops of your chosen essential oil (or essential oils if you want to blend a couple of them) and mix them with a tablespoon of good quality vegetable cold-pressed oil (for example coconut oil, olive oil, or avocado oil). Add the mixture to your bath once it's full. Stir well and enjoy the power of aromas! I very often get asked which essential oils to use with healing baths or showers. If you are using a shower, you can just sprinkle a few drops of your chosen essential oils around your bathroom. Usually it depends on my mood and whether I wish to relax and go to sleep, or maybe relax in order to feel more energized afterwards.

To sum up - for deep relaxation, I prefer to use essential oils like lavender, verbena, ylang-ylang or bergamot.
If however, I need some refreshment and want to energize my mind and soul, I prefer to choose essential oils like lemon, grapefruit, tea tree or eucalyptus.

I also find that a dip in the sea or ocean works in the same way. It is cleansing and freeing. Although you should be wary of polluted areas, because this may counteract the effect.

2. Light is a great method used to cleanse the aura. Light visualization is easy to do. I prefer to use this method out in the sunlight to double the effect, but it can be done indoors as well.

- Lie down in a comfortable place. Take a few cleansing breaths and close your eyes.

- When you are completely relaxed, visualize a white light above you. I use the sunlight that permeates my eyelids, but use whichever works for you. Feel the light come into your body, filling every inch of it.

- As it engulfs your body, imagine it taking the place of negative energy. Imagine the light cleansing and repairing the entirety of your body. Relish in the moment.

- After you have done this for a while, visualize extending the light outside of your body. See it pushing out all of the negative energy. Feel all of your negative energy leaving your body and moving far away from you. The light has now restored your energy and replaced all negativity.

3. Deep breathing exercises are very cleansing for your aura. This one is simple by nature, but it's sometimes tricky to get the hang of. The more you practice, the easier it will become. One very important thing - switch off your mobile device and any other technology around you before you do this.

4. Once a day, find a quiet spot where you will be undisturbed. At first, do this exercise in 5 to 10 minute increments, and then work up to half-hour sessions.

- You should sit comfortably and close your eyes. Start by inhaling for four seconds. Exhale for four seconds. Each time you inhale, feel the breath penetrate deep down into your stomach.

- Concentrate on your breathing as you to this. You are focusing attention only on the inhale and the exhale of your breath. Every time you get distracted, simply redirect your attention to your breath. Continue this process until you are fully relaxed.

- After a few minutes, each time you inhale, imagine that you are inhaling a white, glowing flow of energy. As the breath enters your body, imagine that you are filled with a glowing white light. Feel the light restoring your body and your energy.

- Upon exhaling, see your breath coming out as dark negative energy. Experience the feeling of relief as you push out negative energy.

- Each time your lungs empty, experience a peace knowing that your energy is balanced.

5. Use a sage stick for smudging away negative energy. It is an ancient cleansing process that sounds "hocus-pocus-y," but really works. Simply purchase one at a new age or health food store.

- Light one end of the stick. When you see a flame, blow it out, and it should begin to smolder. Swirl stick around yourself as the smoke encircles you.

- The smoke will rid you of bad energy.

6. Crystals work well to cleanse the aura and also to protect it. There is much to learn about the science behind crystals, how to use them in healing, and how they protect the aura. Let me give you a few basic ways that a beginner such as yourself can easily use crystals for cleansing. When in doubt, or for more complicated crystal usage, consult a professional.

- One thing that crystals are great for is to protect a cleansed aura from negative energy. Black tourmaline can be carried with you. Rose quartz is good as well because it substitutes negative energy for positive energy.

- Labradorite keeps people from sucking away at your positive energy. It will protect your aura from being leeched off of by others.

- Amethyst, bloodstone, citrine, and quartz are all great cleansing stones.

- You can use these stones by carrying them on your person, waving them around you through your aura, wearing them on a piece of jewelry, or putting one next to your bed on an altar.

- You can also meditate with a crystal. Here is an easy way for a beginner to practice an aura cleansing. Find a quiet place and lie down. Practice some deep breathing mediation for a few minutes with your crystal placed on your third eye chakra. Now visualize a white glow coming from the crystal. Allow the light to course through your body, and then around it. Let the light purify your aura as it encircles your body in a cleansing glow. Do this until you feel refreshed and clean.

- Always cleanse your crystals by soaking them in sea salt overnight.

7. Essential oils are fabulous aura cleansers and are very easy to use. You can create your blends, or choose a single oil to use on your own. Common cleansing oils are lime, juniper, cinnamon, cypress, and lemon.

- Make your own aura misting cleanser by using a clean spray bottle, filling it with a cup of spring water, and adding a couple of drops of the essential oil of your choice. Mix it well and spray around your house.

- You can add a few drops of essential oils to a cleansing bath.

- My favorite way though is aromatherapy self-massage. I do it once or twice a day, usually after having a shower. I don't use any artificial skin products. I prefer to take care of my skin with coconut oil, and I add a few drops of my chosen essential oil. The basic rule for self-massage is to mix a few drops of your chosen essential oil with a tablespoon of vegetable oil (coconut, avocado, argan, hazelnut, choose what works for you). Gently massage the mixture into your skin. Focus on your feet, solar plexus, and neck. Inhale the aroma left on your fingers with slow, deep breaths while you imagine your aura brightening as you inhale, and negativity exiting with your exhale. After each aromatherapy massage session, remember to wash your hands. Also make sure you get acquainted with aromatherapy precautions and pick up a good brand of essential oils. Make sure to choose natural and organic oils.

I have written a couple of books specifically on aromatherapy and essential oils. If you are interested in mastering this ancient therapy, you may be interested in picking up one of my booklets from my Holistic Wellness Spa at Home series: (www.amazon.com/author/mtuchowska)

Those are many practical, everyday ways you can easily cleanse your aura. How can you tell if your methods work? You will feel cleansed, at ease, of sound mind, and positive... back to yourself.

You do not have to do them every day, but consistency is key. Find what works best for you. If you do not feel like these methods are working for you, I encourage you to see someone who specializes in aura or energy healing.

One of my favorite things to do as a quick energy fix is to listen to some nice relaxation music (I love ambient music and all kinds of meditation, yoga, and spa music) and go for a quick walk out in nature. A couple of years ago, I made a decision to move outside the city, and it was one of the best things I have ever done for myself. But even if you are a city person, you can still find a park to go to.

I'm very frequently asked what to do when forced to deal with negative people. I know it can be really hard, but here are the best tips I could ever give you:

-Breathe and listen to them.

-Keep a gentle smile on your face. When you smile, your physiology changes and it's almost impossible to feel angry, sad, or depressed.

-Be empathic towards those people. Tell them that "you understand". You see, many people are negative as they have been rejected or deep inside they need someone who can help them.

-As soon as you can, leave the room and go somewhere where you will be alone. Perform a few "dry-clean" movements with your hand. It's like as if you were cleaning your clothes and skin from imaginary dust. Then, if you can, wash your hands with water and soap. You can also shake your hands.

-Before and after dealing with negative people, perform this grounding exercise. Imagine that your feet are like strong roots of a big tree. Close your eyes and imagine the tree growing bigger and bigger.

-Perform a simple prayer and ask the Universe or God for positive energy and emotional balance.

-Choose your favorite essential oil and place a couple of drops on your wrists. Breathe in the aroma and try to relax.

-Finally, try to re-define yourself. Don't fear negative people. Work on your empathy. Your mission is to help them change something in their lives. Pay them back with love, smiles, and assistance as much as you can.

All of the good energy that you put in towards other people will surely come back to you. Nothing gets lost in this Universe.

CHAPTER 5 The Scientific Explanations of Auras

As with many things in the metaphysical world, there is a world of controversy surrounding auras. Many people believe that if something cannot be scientifically proven, it is not real. Yet when things are beyond explanation, and they actually work for you, they are real. For thousands of years people of every descent have believed whole-heartedly in things that they could not explain nor touch. Why now does something need to be scientifically proven to gain validity? So many people are missing out from highly beneficial lifestyles, treatments, and higher-level thinking all in the name of "science."

A Russian couple, the Kirlians, came up with a type of technology that, at one time, was thought to scientifically prove the existence of auras. Kirlian Cameras were thought to be able to "photograph" auras, when in actuality, the "auras" seen are essentially caused by moisture levels, humidity, levels of barometric pressure, voltage, and many other variables.

This "technology" has been scientifically disproven, yet these cameras are still used. Ironically, one of the most famous tests thought to prove that auric energy appears in this type of photography is the same type of test that actually disproved it. A leaf was photographed whole, and then was torn and re-photographed. In the second photograph, the leaf was still shown as whole. The claim was that the second photo showed the aura of the leaf. It was later disproven. The "phantom" effect was simply caused by the electrical discharge from the moisture left behind. If the moisture residue is completely cleaned off before being photographed a second time, there is no "phantom" effect.

Another type of aura photography, the kind seen at "psychic fairs," has also been shown to be false. These aura photographers require that you set your hands onto metal plates that are attached to a black box-like contraption. A Polaroid is then taken by a camera attached to the whole apparatus. Your picture appears with colors around you.

In all actuality, the plates are a galvanometer that gauges skin resistance. There are LED lights that are in the black box that are lit up to different levels of intensity and the colors put on top of your picture. If you had your picture taken twice, once with damp hands and once with dry, the pictures would be totally different.

One possible scientifically-related *theory* is that synesthesia could be responsible for what was thought to be people's ability to see auras. Synesthesia is basically a condition where the sensory-processing centers of the brain are seemingly crossed. They have an overload of synaptic connections. This causes them to have their senses crossed. Some report to see and taste noise or music, visualize or feel tasting something, or even see a color when looking at other people. So the conclusion of a small part of the scientific community is that synesthesia could be easily confused with the ability to see auras.

We all know that the universe and everything in it has been scientifically proven to be full of energy. Then why exactly do most people think that "to see is to believe?" There are plenty of things that we believe to be scientifically proven, but still cannot see. At one point in time, they had not yet even been scientifically proven, but people still believed. The secret to unlocking the connection between the spiritual and the physical is to look at it the opposite way, "to believe is to see."

BONUS CHAPTER
Free Preview of My Book: "Reiki and Reiki Meditation"

Reiki Exercise for Wellness

This exercise starts by you making yourself comfortable. You can either sit or lie on your back with eyes closed. The key is to pay attention to your breathing while following its rhythm. Observe how your breathing flows in and out.

Next, place your hands on the area of your body where you feel tension, or wherever you feel drawn to. In this step, you should be able to make use of your intuition in locating the area of your body that needs relaxation.

The next step is to direct your breath repeatedly and consciously to the affected area of your body. The key is to imagine your breath as the life force energy that flows incessantly through you. Imagine collecting your breath and energy and expanding it into your hands. You will feel the energy spreading out from your hands throughout the other parts of your body. Remain in this position for at least five minutes.

Then, put your hands on another area of your body. Breathe into your hands and repeat steps one through three. You may notice that your breathing changes as you switch positions. This means that the stored experiences and memories in your body are now awakened. You may feel the energy better if you allow yourself to go with the flow.

After going through other areas of your body, open your eyes slowly. Stretch and return to natural consciousness. This exercise will provide you the feeling of calmness. It can also make you more focused and relaxed.

Reiki Exercises for Health

Quick Energizer Method - This Reiki exercise is intended to replenish depleted energy. It aims to provide you with the feeling of being refreshed and of having renewed energy.

The first step is to sit or lie down in a comfortable place. Place one of your hands over the third chakra or the Solar Plexus with the other directly touching your stomach.

Next, relax your hands while closing your eyes. Let your mind rest. Remain in this position for about 10-15 minutes.

After this exercise, you will feel refreshed and rejuvenated with ample energy.

Sleeping Aid

This Reiki exercise for health is intended for individuals who have trouble sleeping at night. It will encourage deep sleep and relaxation.

The first step is to lie on your back or your side or simply be in your normal sleeping position. Put one of your hands on your forehead while the other is left on your stomach. Take note of your stomach expanding up and down as you breathe.

Remain in this position for at least 10 minutes or as long as you like for the Reiki energy to flow. As you feel more relaxed, you will eventually fall asleep.

Reiki Exercise for Self-healing

This exercise makes use of meditation through the Reiki principles. It is intended for inviting good health, clarity, and peace of mind, and for curing illnesses.

The first step is to allow yourself to sit comfortably in an area where your feet are flat on the floor. You can also do a lotus or half-lotus position.

Next, cross both of your hands over your heart. You can also press your fingers and palms together in front of your heart.

Then, say these Reiki principles out loud: "Just for today (1) Do not be irate, (2) Do not be worried, (3) Be grateful (4) Work hard, and (5) Be kind to others.

And... the most important thing: smile and laugh, laugh and smile. It's free. Always has been and always will be!

Now, like I promised, I will share with you certain Reiki tools I have developed as a part of my Reiki courses experiences (1-2 level). They will equip you with more healing strategies, plus, in case you are thinking of doing a Reiki attunement, you will feel more or less prepared. Again, this is something that I was taught and that I adjusted to my lifestyle and developed with personal practice.

You may think of it as a recipe book. Some people buy recipe books looking for specific recipes that they want to follow through. Some people get cookbooks as they are looking for inspiration, variety, and flavors they can apply in their kitchen the way they want. Both attitudes are awesome. It really depends on you and how you want your Reiki journey to be. If you find it easier just to follow though, then follow through. If you prefer to use my guidance as a template to create your own way, feel free to do so. Simply do whatever feels right for you right now...

Reiki for quick self-healing: hand positions

After connecting to Reiki and purifying your energy field using Ken'Yoku, you may proceed to practicing the following self-healing rituals. If you don't have time to go through the whole Ken'Yoku process from chapter 4, that's fine. Simply put the intention and do it quickly in your mind. Simply think that you want and need to connect to Reiki and be grateful for this amazing healing opportunity. You may also try to practice it on others by simply giving it the right intention. Simply do what I do and observe your body, mind, and spirit! Personally, I love the following self-healing techniques when I am in bed, ready to go to sleep, sometimes before an occasional nap, or first thing in the morning, when I am still in bed. It's kind of a prayer also!

Hands over your eyes

Hands over your jaw, thumbs under your ears

Hands on the back of your head, on your cranium, above the occipital bone

Left hand on your occipital bone and right hand above it

Both hands around your neck or on your throat (balancing the throat chakra and unleashing unlimited creativity)

Hands on your sternum (helps alleviate anxiety)

Right hand on your forehead, left hand on your occipital bone (great for creating new habits and getting rid of negative thoughts, emotions and also addictions)

Both hands on the top of your head, making sure all your chakras remain balanced and mentally energized

Preview the book on Amazon:

http://www.amazon.com/dp/B00VCEEMES

CONCLUSION:Living a Peaceful and Balanced Life

Life is a journey that we are all on. In order to make the most of it, it is of the utmost importance to live holistically balanced in order to achieve holistic wellness. The energy of the universe is alive in all of us, and we are alive in it. Everyone plays a part in each other's existence. If you want to be a beneficial element, radiating healthy, vibrant energy, it is important to learn how to understand and feel our own energy in order to see how it has an effect on our own health, circumstances, and relationships.

Now that you know the basics on aura and energy, I urge you to get started! You see the need for holistic wellness and energy balanced in your life and how necessary it is. Your energy must be balanced and your aura bright and healthy in order to maintain healthy, meaningful relationships. Use the tools and information provided to enrich your life in all areas.

Practice the methods of aura cleansing. Keep up with further investigation. See an energy healer! Use the techniques for seeing energy and auras to focus and hone your skills! Remember, do not become discouraged. It takes time and practice, like anything else worth achieving.

Spending time in worry, self-doubt, anxiety, and depression can now be a part of your past. It no longer takes precedence in your present moment, nor in your future. You can attain peace and calm in your life, investing only minutes a day!

You are the captain of your own ship. No longer will you be a slave to circumstance! Do not spend another day wondering, "Why me?" You will have positive energy coursing through your body, enabling positive thoughts, actions, and attracting great things for yourself!

Do not waste any more time and energy being dead weight! Do not sit another day in a spiritual body that is unwell! There is no need to as long as you continue to search for knowledge on how to see, utilize, and make the most of the universal energy we are filled with and a part of. Your spirit will be energized, your body healed, and your relationships fulfilled.

I wish you the best of luck in your spiritual journey!

Finally, if you have a few seconds, I would like you to ask you to do me a little favor. Please post your honest review on Amazon. Share your thoughts with other customers and readers. If you think that my book is helpful, please share it with your family and friends.

If you happen to have any questions or simply want to say "hi", e-mail me at:

info@holisticwellnessproject.com

For more inspiration and empowerment visit my blog www.HolisticWellnessProject.com

There is also a free complimentary eBook waiting for you.

"Holistically Productive" will inspire you to create a productive, yet stress-free lifestyle full of vibrant health, happiness and abundance.

Visit: www.holisticwellnessproject.com/free-ebook/giveaway.html

And grab your free copy of "Holistically Productive" now (available both as pdf and mobi). You will also be notified about my new releases and I'll make sure that you receive all my new books for free or 99c.

I wish you health and balance,

Marta

Marta's books and courses (wellness, health, personal development, spa, natural therapy, healthy recipes and much much more):

www.amazon.com/author/mtuchowska

www.AlkalineDietLifestyle.com

www.holisticwellnessproject.com/personal-development-books/

Finally, I would love to keep in touch with you for years to come!

Let's connect:

www.facebook.com/HolisticWellnessProject

www.instagram.com/marta_wellness

www.pinterest.com/MartaWellness/

www.twitter.com/Marta_Wellness

www.linkedin.com/in/MartaTuchowska

www.goodreads.com/author/show/7520321.Marta_Tuchowska

Made in the USA
San Bernardino, CA
25 January 2018